Bookosmia
For Kids, By kids

Published in 2023 by Bookosmia - India's No.1 publisher 'For kids, By kids'.
www.bookosmia.com


ISBN: 9789360453541

Author : Aashritha Surya Prakash | Illustrator : Pooja Saklani | Editor : Sara Batool

This book belongs to :

..................................................

..................................................

*To my amma, Ragha Sudha, who inculcated in me, at an early age, a deep love for literature, writing, and our itihasas and puranas; those bedtime stories with Hanuman were the best part of my day!*

*To my appa, Surya Prakash, who always supported me no matter what and inspires me to think from everyone's perspective in an unbiased way.*

*To my brother Ananth, who was the first person to hear my stories. Without you, this would not have been possible.*

*To my grandparents and my family, who told me stories from the vast repertoire of the Mahabharata and Ramayana; one of my first exposures to the beauty of sharing this textbook for life.*

*To Vardhini ma'am and Archana ma'am, who kindled the spark lit by my family, teaching me the ins and outs of using writing, podcasting, and publishing as a way to express myself.*

*To all the teachers I have ever had, you helped me become the person I am today.*

*-Aashritha Surya Prakash*

# Author's note

They say that every action has a reaction, but what if the action itself is a reaction?

When we talk about personalities, we describe them as 'bad' or 'good'. However, life isn't like that. We have different shades to our personalities.

With this book, I aim to show that nobody is completely bad or good. Those who are perceived as completely good, like Yudishtira, do have a hidden vice: for example, he had a very difficult relationship with the game of dice. On the other side of the coin, people like Shakuni exist. He is perceived as evil and seems to have all the typical characteristics of a villain: he opposes and despises the protagonists and supports the 'bad' side. However, he does have virtues: his undying love for his sister and his complete loyalty to his father even though he is deceased.

I believe one of the most fundamental lessons I learnt from the Mahabharata is that you cannot judge a book by its cover. No, hear me out. I know it's been said a million times before, but this is validated by this epic story particularly.

The Mahabharata's most fundamental characters (which, let's be honest, are ALL the characters), like any character, have their own back stories. Their childhoods and early lives are seen through their adult personalities and decisions.

For example, having had a childhood full of comparisons between him and his brother, Dhritarashtra has an eternal sense of unfulfillment and an inferiority complex.

He then projects his fears through his son, going so far as to imbue him with these negative qualities. However, in the midst of all this lies a small glimmer of virtue: Dhritarashtra's unquestioning love for his son, Duryodhana.

Hopefully, I have managed to convey these emotions and thoughts through this endeavor.

# *Mahabharata family tree*

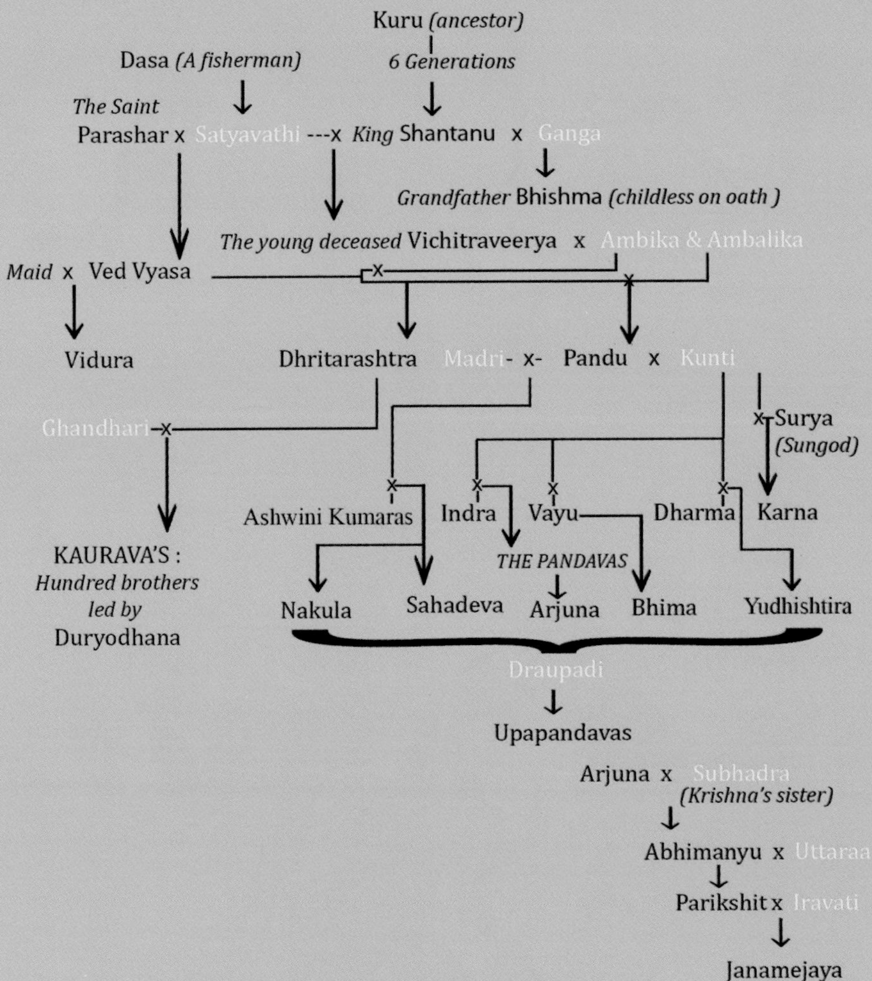


**To read a synopsis of the Mahabharata please turn to page 85*

# UNHEARD VOICES OF MAHABHARATA

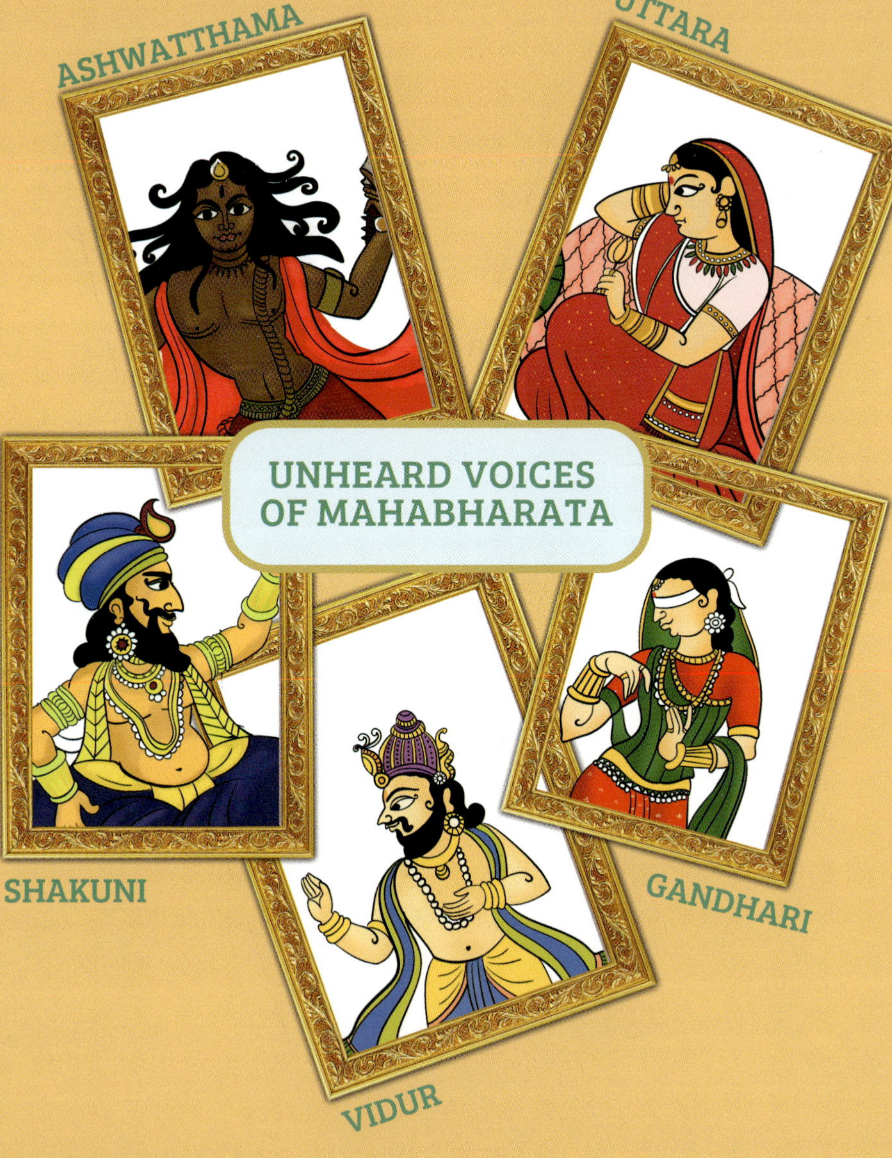

**Many say....**

"He knowingly sided with the wrong side in the war."

"He was evil and enjoyed seeing others suffer."

"He was a spoiled and talentless boy."

***But what is his real story?***

# Ashwatthama

As the 18th day of the great war of Kurukshetra commenced, a handsome young man put on his armour, fit for a king, knowing fully well that this was going to be one of the most trying days of his life. Two days ago, his father Dronacharya, guru(teacher) of the Pandavas' and Kauravas', had been brutally and unjustly murdered by Drishtadyumna, son of Draupada and a close ally of the Pandavas. He had taken an oath to avenge the death of his father, which he was yet to fulfil.

The sun rose as the young man, Ashwatthama, looked out onto the battlefield, eager to fight. He saw how the very sky seemed to be tainted with the blood of the warriors who had died the most honourable death for a Kshatriya man: a death on the battlefield. He looked out over the battlefield, contemplating the choices he had made throughout his life, which had led to this fateful day.

* * * * * * * * * * * *

In the time of yore, two young boys from very different backgrounds befriended each other during their long and strenuous education; Drona, the son of a sage and Draupada, the son of a king. During these eighteen years, they formed a close bond, which they recalled fondly just before leaving the ashram.

*"During my years here, I have gained many things: immense knowledge and a kingdom. I am now old and fit enough to rule. However, the greatest thing I have gained is your friendship! Your friendship is of more value to me than the great kingdom of Panchaal which is my inheritance. Dear friend Drona, the years I have spent with you are some of the best in my life. I shall always love, cherish and remember you."*

*"Likewise, brother Draupada, likewise. "*

*"If you ever need anything, anything at all, come to my court where I will gladly part with half my kingdom for you."*

*"Your words, brother Draupada, are enough."*

Many, many years later, Panchaal was a flourishing kingdom. Its capital and harem were the envy of all the kingdoms that made up the great continent of Bharatvarsha.

King Draupada was a just and kind leader. He took care of both the economical and political needs of his people as well as their social and cultural needs. He built temples and banquet halls while still waging wars.

Meanwhile, Drona got married to Kripi, the sister of Rishi Kripa. Together, they had a beautiful little son they called Ashwatthama. On his forehead, Ashwatthama had a divine jewel that prevented him from experiencing hunger or sickness. They didn't have much and struggled to make ends meet, but lived a simple and contented life.

One day, Ashwatthama, who many said was the split image of his father, was playing in the ashrama when he heard the other boys describing the creamy and rich taste of milk. Running into the house, he asked his mother,

*"Mother, my friends describe a creamy and special drink called milk. They say it is like amrita (nectar). What is this milk, Mother, and may I taste it?"*

An astonished Kripi did not know what to do. Since they were too poor to afford milk, she mixed rice flour with water and gave it to her son. The innocent little child drank the solution and started jumping around happily. He ran out of the house and excitedly told his friends that he had tasted milk! Kripi watched him silently, tears sliding down the bridge of her nose and falling upon her cheeks. She wept sorrowfully at his unwavering trust and her deception.

When her husband came home later with the alms he had collected, Kripi broke down and told him everything.

A defeated Drona decided enough was enough and decided to forgo his pride and ask his old friend, now king of Panchaal, King Draupada, for help.

The next day, when King Draupada was holding court, a simply-adorned old Brahman entered the court. Unlike the others, he did not bow low to the king or praise him, but instead addressed him directly.

*"Brother Draupada, it is I, Drona who has returned! I have come to remind you of a promise you made in our youth: you said you would part with half your kingdom if ever I asked. Now, however, being older and wiser, I know not to ask for such a gift. I ask instead, for something quite meagre in comparison: a cow. Grant me this, then, to honour the oath you took, so many years ago."*

At this bold request, the entire court started whispering. How could this man, a poor Brahman, ever suggest that their beloved and noble king was indebted to him? The arrogance!

Meanwhile, King Draupada was in a dilemma. What was he to do? Should he honour his oath and give his friend a cow, while bringing down his social status in the process, or should he turn him away? While the latter protected his pride, wasn't it one of the greatest sins: to not honour an oath? Eventually, he decided on a middle path.

*"I shall grant you the cow, O Brahman if you agree you have come here for alms. Don't expect me to give you a cow on pretences of friendship, for friendship can exist only between equals. You can go to the treasury right now, where they are giving alms. I will make sure you get enough to lead a happy, peaceful, and contented life."*

Hearing this speech in that once beloved voice, Dronacharya stormed out of the court, yelling,

*"You will see Draupada! One day, I will be your equal and will attain the status required to gain your friendship!"*

✶✶✶✶✶✶✶✶✶✶✶

Enraged at Draupada's crude and vain insult, Drona now sought the help of his brother-in-law, Kripacharya, who was working as a tutor to the Kaurava and Pandava princes. He suggested that Drona, an accomplished warrior, should take the post of martial arts and warfare teacher for the princes.

Driven by love and desire for his family to have a better life, Drona decided to visit the palace and enquire.

As he neared the palace, he saw a group of boys gathered around a well. He walked closer to the well and saw that they were arguing.

*"Boys, what is the matter and why are you arguing?"*

*"Bhima here has thrown our ball into the well! I told him to throw lighter but I guess he just doesn't know his own strength. Come on!"*

Realising these were the Kuru princes, Drona decided to impress them with his skills.

*"OK. Just watch me and I'll get your ball back from the well. Do you have an arrow?"*

The boys shook their heads.

*"OK then. Get me a few strong stems of Kusha grass."*

Kusha stems clutched in their chubby fists, the boys returned minutes later. Choosing the longest and strongest of the stems, Drona shot it with such exact force that it hit the side of the ball, causing it to bounce to the other side of the well and spring into Drona's hand.

Amazed by this show of skill, Yudishtira decided to test the man further. He said he had once lost his ring in the well and hadn't been able to retrieve it. Without a word, he took the remaining blades of grass and made notches with the grass. He took some cow dung nearby and stuck it to the end of the notch. Throwing it into the well, the ring got stuck in the cow dung. He then threw the remaining blades with such precision that they got stuck to one another, becoming a rope. Pulling it out, he got the ring from the cow dung and offered it to Yudishtira.

*"But now it's so dirty! Such an expensive ring, covered in mud and cow dung?"*

Drona made an umbrella of arrows over the boys and used the Varuna Astra (the weapon of Varuna, the god of water) to cause it to rain. He collected the rain water in a coconut shell, washed the ring, and gave it back to Yudishtira.

Amazed, Arjuna enquired about this talented stranger's identity. Laughing, Drona told Arjuna to ask his grand-uncle Bhishma. Instantly realising who this was, Bhishma Pitamaha asked Drona, henceforth called Dronacharya, to be the boys' royal warfare tutor. Glad that his goal was achieved, Drona accepted.

As his new job required Drona to live at the palace, he moved into the palace with his wife and son. Since his son was roughly the same age and same status as the princes (being their guru's son) the boys grew up together. Ashwatthama thought Duryodhana to be more powerful and chose to befriend him over the Pandavas.

Growing up, Duryodhana held Ashwatthama even above his brothers. Ashwatthama was his closest ally, his best friend, his most trusted advisor and confidant. Ashwatthama loved Duryodhana back and saw him as the brother he never had.

✶✶✶✶✶✶✶✶✶✶✶

The sounds of a man in agony being their guide, three armour-clad men fought their way through the tangled nest of branches surrounding a once crystal-clear and serene pool of water that was now tinged red with blood. A once-esteemed and kingly figure now lay with blood pouring from his thighs near this pool of water, clearly close to death. When they reached this pool, one of the men broke down in tears at the sight of this beloved friend; their dear comrade, utterly and completely broken. Seeing this, the fallen friend, Duryodhana, consoled his weeping comrade.

*"I will attain moksha, Ashwatthama, having died a noble death worthy of a warrior on the glorious battlefield of Kurukshetra. Meanwhile, the Pandavas will sit on a throne of skeletons and rule over a kingdom of widows. While I attain eternal peace, they will struggle and toil for a lost cause: to bring peace and joy back to a barren kingdom.*

*"Do you know how I ended up in this state? Bhima challenged me to a mace duel to end the war. My mother, Gandhari, offered to make me invincible. By casting her holy chaste gaze upon me, my body would be hard as a diamond. I had been told to bathe in the Ganga and come to her the way I had been born. As I got out of the river, Krishna saw me and mocked me, advising me to cover the area from my navel to my thighs. I fell for his advice but this made the covered body parts around the thigh vulnerable and not protected by my mother's holy gaze. Following the cowherd Krishna's directions, Bhima broke the rule of Malla yudha (Mace duel) by breaking my thighs. Now, I appoint you, Ashwatthama, the last commander of the Kaurava army. Here are your orders: Take Kripa and Kritavarma and avenge my death!"*

✶✶✶✶✶✶✶✶✶✶✶

Around Ashwatthama, there was a cry of joy as the Pandava camp celebrated the death of their hated rival and their victory in the great Kurukshetra war, but a burning mindless rage consumed his entire being. His vision became blurry as he let out a bellow of fury that shook the very earth.

Amid the volcano of rage, a fountain of brotherly love and defensiveness poured. This fountain of love cleared his mind and poured forth a flow of thoughts.

How could they have done this to Duryodhana? That man, lying on the crude forest floor had once laid down on the softest and finest mattresses in the kingdom! That angel in disguise had given Ashwatthama shelter, fed him, and filled his heart with love! No, he would not let it end this way.

He fixed his mind on one, and only one motive that he would work with steely, single-minded devotion: to avenge the death of the man who had taken him and his family in during their time of need, and had even granted Ashwatthama the honour of being his friend.

Driven by this cause, Ashwatthama devised a plan of revenge, one so devious and underhanded, he was to regret it for the rest of his life. After hearing it, they say the very trees were so repulsed, they drew their long, slender, blood-stained branches away from him.

However repulsive the plan was, Kripa and Kritavarma were bound by their oaths of loyalty to their king. The three men slowly crept towards where the Pandavas were camping on the outskirts of the battlefield as per tradition.

Later, a Nishada (forest dweller) would tell everybody about how he saw three men walking through the forest. One walked carefully and stealthily, like a hunter stalking his prey. One was pale and trembling, and walked cautiously and guiltily. Another walked with the gait of a man resigned to his fate.

The three men avoided or silently murdered the guards and walked into the camp. They saw one of the tents had its flap open and peered into the tent. In the dim light of the oil lamp, they saw 6 figures sleeping. Assuming them to be the Pandavas and their commander, Dhrishtadyumna, they moved slowly into the tent, and a small battle ensued. By then, a sentry had heard the kerfuffle and raised the alarm, but it was too late. The six people had no chance and were all killed in cold blood. Just then, the oil lamp in the tent was turned over and the tent caught fire! In the light, Ashwatthama saw that it was indeed Dhrishtadyumna, but not the Pandavas.

Instead, the bodies of the five 'Upapandavas', Pandavas' sons by Draupadi, lay on the floor.

Hearing the noise, Draupadi woke up in alarm and stumbled towards her husbands' tent, worrying they were hurt. However, the Pandavas were perfectly fine and were grabbing their weapons to go out and find out what was wrong.

Hours later, they informed a grieving Draupadi that Dhrishtadyumna, her last surviving brother, and her five sons, who she barely spent any time with, were now dead. An enraged Draupadi told her husbands to avenge their sons' deaths.

✶✶✶✶✶✶✶✶✶✶✶

On hearing about the death of the Pandavas' children at the hands of Ashwatthama, Kripa, and Kritavarma, Duryodhana was overwhelmed with emotion.

*"What!? Have we stooped to killing children now? Oh god, I hope I am relieved of these sins! Nevertheless, you, my friend Ashwatthama, have proven you are my greatest ally. At least I die knowing I have such loyal and faithful friends."*

In his last, dying moments, Duryodhana felt remorse for all he had said and done throughout his life. For causing this great war of bloodshed. For widowing and orphaning so many innocent women.

At the death of his king, Ashwatthama went numb with shock. Moments later he began to cry and weep. Eventually, his sorrow was replaced by a thirst for vengeance. He let out a scream of rage that caused the very air to vibrate.

This scream alerted the Pandavas as to his whereabouts. Knowing this, Kripa and Kritavarma ran away from the scene, not wishing to be caught by the Pandavas. On their way there, Krishna told Arjuna that Ashwatthama had the Brahmasheersha astra, the same weapon Arjuna had received from Dronacharya for saving his life from a man-eating crocodile, and was likely to use it.

When the Pandavas discovered Ashwatthama, a terrible and fierce duel ensued. As predicted by Krishna, blinded by his emotions, Ashwatthama released the Brahmasheersha astra. However, having been warned by Krishna, Arjuna immediately released the same astra to counter it.

The power of this astra was so immense that if they collided, it could bring about Pralaya (the end of the world). So, the sages Narada and Vyasa stopped the astras and asked both to recall them. Arjuna obeyed instantly. However, since the astra only obeyed righteous men, it would by no means obey Ashwatthama. His thirst for vengeance not quenched, Ashwatthama said:

*"Maybe the astra will not kill the Pandavas, but it will most definitely kill their descendants! This astra will destroy the unborn child of Abhimanyu, still in Uttara's womb."*

As it whirled towards the women's tent, Subhadra jumped in front of Uttara, her daughter-in-law, and saved the child.

The sacred jewel on Ashwatthama's head was taken by Yudishtira. He was sentenced to an immortal life full of sorrow and pain, from which he would not be rescued even by death and not even a single soul would take pity on him.

Legends say he still wanders the Earth, feeling remorse for his actions and hoping and praying and wishing to be rescued by death.

And thus, what began with a thirst for milk ended with a thirst for blood. Ashwatthama's story teaches us that even though grief is a normal human emotion, we must not let it contort into rage or morph into anger. We must learn to process grief as grief.

**Many say...**

"She didn't play much of a role in the Kuru dynasty."

"She was just a young girl who married into the family."

"She was a meek and shy person who didn't stand up for what was right."

***But what's her real story?***

# Uttaraa

An old woman walked around a palace that she should've felt the pride to own, but which just felt empty without the voices of her family. She was Uttaraa- daughter of Queen Sudeshna and King Virata, at whose court the Pandavas spent a year in concealment during their exile. She was the wife of Abhimanyu, the daughter-in-law of Arjuna.

She walked through the old nursery, where Gandhari had given birth to the Kauravas, where generations of Kuru princes had been born and brought up. She walked out into the gardens, where Drona had first met the Kauravas, where she brought up her son, Parikshit, and her grandson Janamejaya. She walked through the garden that was once the pride and joy of their kingdom due to its magnificence and uniqueness, but now in ruins.

Just like her.

Once, tongues uttered praises in her name every day. Now, she had lost her youthful lustre and was forgotten. Ah, how things had transpired! Such is the irony of life, she thought. We work and work for those few moments of fame, without realising how fickle it is. And when we finally do realise it, we are too old to change anything.

Suddenly, her solitude was interrupted by a voice. A voice dear to her, very similar to that of one dearly departed.

*"Grandmother! Where are you?"*

*"Grandmother! Where are you?"*

At first, she didn't respond, wondering why he had come now. Not hearing an answer, the voice teasingly continued,

*"Ah! Well, if you won't come out, then I guess I'll have to take back all this lemon and mango pickle I made for you. Oh! Looks like the soldiers have also brought the silk sari my queen wanted to give you, and the jewellery that belonged to Queen Draupadi that you were looking for! Well, I guess I'll have to take everything back.....oh yes! I also have to ride...on a horse... for two hours...unfed...from my grandmother's house..."*

*"Oh, don't give me all that! And give me that!"*

The lady playfully snatched everything from the man, a king by the name of Janamejaya.

*"Oh, finally remembered your old grandmother, have you?"*

*"I have told you multiple times to come and stay with us at my palace. There, I can see and placate you every day. But you insist on staying here, deep in the forest, what can I do except come and visit you whenever I can?"*

She shook her head at his response.

*"This is the house of your forefathers! This is where you, your father, and many others grew up. How dare you expect me to leave all this and come and live in that shiny new palace you built for yourself?"*

*"Come now, grandmother. Don't be angry with me. I promise to come and visit you every week. Now will you please make lunch for me?"*

*"Harrumph! Just empty promises as usual."*

Nevertheless, Uttaraa went to the kitchen and started bellowing orders at all the maids to get the kitchen ready so she could cook.

An hour or so later, King Janamejaya and his grandmother Uttaraa were conversing and eating lunch. As the king spoke, Uttaraa got lost in his eyes, so similar to that of her husband. She noticed the subtleties she had failed to notice before. How he ate just like his grandfather. How his lips curled and his head swayed as he playfully teased her. How the look in his eyes was identical to the look she received from his grandfather: one of complete and utter love. Suddenly, she broke down in tears. Seeing her cry so, King Janamejaya was distraught.

*"What happened grandmother?"*

*"It's just...I realised how similar you are to your grandfather, and how my life might have turned out if he was alive."*

*"How do you feel so deeply for a man who died less than a year after he married you, grandmother? Please grandmother, tell me, so I may understand your pain."*

*"Very well..."*

✶✶✶✶✶✶✶✶✶✶✶

Just before monsoon, one evening, Draupadi was in conversation with Yudishtira.

*"Is it wise to go to Hastinapura, Yudishtira? When Duryodhana tried multiple times to get you killed, you somehow escaped. You married me and gained my father, King Draupada, as your ally.*

*Then, when you revealed yourself as alive, he tried to give us Khandavaprastha so that people perceive that he's generous, while giving us nothing. Now, we have built Indraprastha.You know that our castle is the envy of all of Bharata. After all that, he's trying to get rid of us, once and for all! He's just angry and envious of the fact that every time he tried to give us nothing, somehow, we always made something of it."*

*"You know the Shastras state that a king can never refuse an invitation, especially to a dice game, Panchaali."*

*"And you just like playing dice!"*

By noon, the Pandavas had reached the ornate palace in Hastinapura which Duryodhana had built, specifically for this game.

Duryodhana welcomed his guests.

*"Ah! Finally, my...beloved cousins have arrived! At last, we can begin.Yudishtira, I think you will be playing?"*

*"Yes. And I presume that you will be playing Duryodhana?"*

*"No, no, not today. My dear maternal uncle, Shakuni, will be representing us."*

Duryodhana maintained a gracious smile, but in his eyes, a mad light gleamed. The thirst for vengeance sparkling in him. Meanwhile, at this unexpected news, all the blood drained from the Pandavas' faces. They knew Shakuni was a master at dice games.

At first, Yudishtira staked comparatively small items. However, they gradually grew larger. First his silver armband, then his jewelled crown, then the royal treasury, and even his kingdom! When he lost everything, he began staking his brothers, one by one, and eventually himself! He lost everything. Then Duryodhana offered Yudhisthira a deal. If he staked Draupadi and won, then he would give everything back to him. Blinded by a desire to win, he agreed, and...he lost! Triumphant, Duryodhana had Draupadi unwillingly dragged into court and then attempted to disrobe her. Draupadi was saved through divine intervention.

Finally coming to his senses, Dhritarashtra offered her three boons. Using them, she won back everything Yudishtira had lost. Enraged, Duryodhana taunted Yudishtira into accepting a deal:

*"One more round of dice. Winner takes all. Losers have to spend twelve years in exile and one year incognito. If discovered during the thirteenth year, they must repeat their twelve years of exile."*

Ignoring Draupadi's pleas, Yudishtira agreed.

Shakuni rolled the dice...and Yudishtira lost!

✶✶✶✶✶✶✶✶✶✶✶

Watching her grandson listen in rapt attention, Uttaraa smiled in satisfaction.

*"Now, if that doesn't teach you about the dangers of gambling, I don't know what will."*

*"Grandmother, please don't interrupt the story with a lecture!"*

*"It's not a ..."*

*"Either way, I don't gamble!"*

Uttaraa broke into laughter and continued the story.

✶✶✶✶✶✶✶✶✶✶✶

As per the deal, the Pandavas had to spend 12 years in exile and one year incognito before being able to reclaim their kingdom.

Finally, they reached the thirteenth year. They decided to spend it in King Virata's kingdom, Matsya, working at his palace under various aliases. Arjuna took on a curse that had been cast on him by Urvashi and became a eunuch and was Princess Uttaraa's dance and music instructor. Bhima was a cook, Yudhisthira a learned Brahmin, Nakula a groom, and Sahadeva a cowherd. They spent many months in the palace, cleverly eluding capture.

However, during this time, Draupadi's exquisite beauty did not go unnoticed. A man by the name of Kichaka, an army general and brother-in-law of Virata soon became entranced by her beauty. To avoid his relentless attention, Draupadi sought the help of Bhima, who eventually killed him. After his body had been found, everyone suspected Draupadi, who claimed she had five Gandharvas as husbands who were cursed for two more months, but who would always help her when needed.

When news of this reached Hastinapura, the Kauravas realised that the woman with 5 Gandharvas as husbands was probably Draupadi. However, they could not accuse the Pandavas without solid evidence. So, they came up with a plan that would not only give them proof of the Pandavas living there, but would also add Matsya to their growing territory.

One troop was to attack Matsya from the North and steal all of its cows as well as Virata's attention. After a day, the other would attack from the South and conquer it.

The first troop succeeded and the second attacked. Since all his soldiers were in the North, only the young prince Uttarakumara was left. Taking Arjuna as his charioteer, he bravely rode toward the army. However, at the last moment, his nerves failed him. Taking Arjuna's help, he defeated the Kauravas. Seeing Arjuna, the Kauravas now had definite proof that the Pandavas had been hiding in Matsya for a year. But there was a slight catch. The year had been over two months ago! The dejected Kauravas went back to Hastinapura.

When King Virata found out about the Pandavas' true identities and how they had helped him, he offered Arjuna his daughter Uttaraa's hand in marriage. However, Arjuna refused since she was his pupil and offered his son Abhimanyu's hand in marriage instead!

✶✶✶✶✶✶✶✶✶✶✶

*"And that is how I met your grandfather! Uttaraa exclaimed with a twinkle in her eye."*

*"But how could you just marry a man who you hadn't met?" said an outraged Janamejaya.*

*"Later, they showed me a few portraits of him and believe me when I say that after that I didn't complain. I fell in love with his strong chin and dashing smile the moment I saw him."*

*"You still haven't told me how he died."*

*"Impatient as mustard seeds bubbling in oil you are! I'll get there when I get there."*

*"And when will that be?"*

Uttaraa silenced him with a glare and continued.

✶✶✶✶✶✶✶✶✶✶✶

Even though they had now fulfilled the terms of the deal, Duryodhana refused to give the Pandavas even a needlepoint of land. They sent messengers, peacemakers, sages, and even Krishna to persuade Duryodhana into resolving this petty family feud without innocent people dying. Eventually, Duryodhana sent them a formal declaration of war. Both sides prepared for a war that was prophesied to bring about the end of the Dwapara yuga, the third of the four yugas (unit of time) where one yuga comprises 1,00,000 years.

Before the war, Bhishma was appointed as commander. He promised Duryodhana that he would kill ten thousand Pandava soldiers every day, but would not touch the Pandavas. When he fell on the tenth day, Duryodhana had to choose a new commander.

On the morning of the eleventh day, Duryodhana was in a dilemma and sought help from his dear friend, Karna, King of Anga. Karna thought long and hard and suggested Drona. Overwhelmed, Drona agreed and offered Duryodhana a boon as desired by him. Immediately, Duryodhana exclaimed,

*"I want Yudhishtira brought to me in chains."*

That day, Drona tried his best to fulfil his word, but couldn't make it close to Yudhisthira as Arjuna, who had caught wind of his plans, had sent four commanders of their army to guard him.

*"I said, I wanted Yudisthira captured alive. Is this the extent of your prowess, o commander?" goaded Duryodhana*

*"If you can lure Arjuna away, it will come to pass." retorted Drona calmly.*

When Drona had gotten past all defences and was on the verge of capturing him, he heard the distinctive sound of the Panchajanya. He looked around in horror and saw Krishna driving the horses wildly as Arjuna, eyes blazing with hatred, killed thousands of warriors with a single arrow. At that exact moment, a lightning bolt flashed just behind Arjuna, striking the soldiers behind him and killing them.

That night, a council of war was held by the Kauravas. Duryodhana reproached his commander, Drona, who, angered by the slander, retaliated.

*"I came so close to capturing Yudishtira today. But Arjuna, who was your responsibility, appeared. As I said before, if you want me to make good on my promise to capture Yudhisthira, you must make good on yours and distract Arjuna."*

There were great losses on both sides on the twelfth day. Both lost many, many soldiers. The Pandavas lost many great heroes; Satyajit, Sataanika, and Vrika, to name a few. The Kauravas lost almost all of one of their largest battalions: the Trigarta army.

On the thirteenth day, Arjuna was attacked by the remainder of the Trigarta army. Despite being irritated, he could not refuse and was drawn away from Yudishtira, sincerely apologising for leaving his side at this critical time.

Drona then arranged his army in the impenetrable chakra vyuha, a multi-tiered defence formation that was almost impossible to breach.

The Pandavas were stunned as only Arjuna could break through it. At that moment, 16-year-old Abhimanyu, one of Arjuna's sons came forward and revealed that when he was in his mother's womb, his father had revealed how to enter the chakra vyuha, but not how to come out of it. So he could make a breach but couldn't come out. Yudishtira assured him that they would hold the breach open until he came out.

In the first layer of the vyuha, everything went well. Abhimanyu went in while the Pandavas dutifully held it open. Then they reached the second layer which consisted of the Sindhu king Jayadratha and his army. Long ago, the Pandavas had humiliated Jayadratha. Determined to get revenge, he performed an austere penance to Shiva and was blessed with a boon that he would defeat them at least once. This boon was now coming into effect.

Meanwhile, Abhimanyu continued, unaware of the mortal danger he was in. Drona, Kripa, Ashwatthama, Dushasana's son Laxman, Karna, and Kritavarma attacked Abhimanyu. They killed his charioteer and broke his carriage.

First, they fought with bows and arrows. The six warriors turned all of Abhimanyu's bows and arrows into dust. Then he jumped out of his crumbling carriage and unsheathed the sword. Drona cut the sword blade from the hilt. In desperation, the brave boy picked up his chariot wheel which was promptly shattered into a hundred different fragments. Abhimanyu picked up the mace and duelled with Laxman. In the course of the duel, both of them fainted out of exhaustion. Returning to consciousness first, Laxman killed Abhimanyu in one swift stroke. The six warriors who had all sworn to be righteous before the war, four out of whom were Maharathis meaning master warriors, were now dancing around the broken body of a 16-year-old boy like a vulture circles its prey, cackling like hyenas.

✶✶✶✶✶✶✶✶✶✶✶✶

Uttaras' tears rolled down her pearl-like cheeks.

*"When I got the news, I was pregnant with your father. I fell on the ground rolling in pain, feeling as though my heart was ripped out of my chest, screaming like a mad person, wishing, waiting, wanting to die. Only the thought of my unborn child, the carrier of his father's blood, kept me alive. After I returned to the palace, I focused all my energies on raising my child, who was now the only heir to the throne.*

*When the Pandavas handed over the throne to him and decided to go on the holy journey to attain heaven, I lost one of my biggest supporters: my mother-in-law Draupadi. Then, one day, your father, my son, Parikshit was hunting in the forest when he asked the sage for some water. Being deep in meditation, the sage did not answer. Angered, he put a dead snake around the sage's neck. A disciple of the sage who witnessed this c..c..cursed your father to d...die of a snake bite in seven days. At that time, you were only a baby. On the seventh day, your father bit into an apple and found a worm which expanded into a snake named Takshaka who wanted to take revenge on our family for burning his home while building Indraprastha. He...he died of the bite. Now, I had lost my life's goal. I then set all my energies on raising you and helping your mother. Now see where I am? In an old palace, recounting my life's stories to my grandson.*

*Sometimes I still wonder if I had pampered your father too much. Maybe that's why he became so arrogant and brought about his demise. If only he was still here. He might've - he might've been able to see the great empire you've built."*

At this, her grandson Janamejaya had no words. He had defeated thousands of soldiers and endured many hardships - all without shedding a tear. Now, however, he was on his knees with his hands around his grandmother's, feeling more emotions than anyone could comprehend.

Even though he had finally got answers to questions he had been asking for years, he felt hollow. He felt so deeply for his grandmother, a woman who had experienced more pain than should be possible for a person. In his eyes, she was the bravest person in his life. Even though Abhimanyu had died, he had gone to heaven. His grandmother, on the other hand, had suffered a fate worse than hell, while still raising his father and enduring slights and insults. And he never knew. Such is the pain of so many wonderful women, whose tales remain untold and unknown. Even now, all they do is selflessly give and give. So many women like his grandmother had experienced and endured so much pain and sadness, in silence. As long as these tales remain untold, the world will be shrouded in the veil of ignorance, he thought.

And thus, the innocent and bubbly maiden faced the harsh, harsh world. And she faced it all with maturity far beyond her age. Her story is a shining example of how resilience does pay off if you are focused.

**Many say ...**

"He was cold-blooded."

"He found joy in ruining others for fun."

"He had no reasons for his actions."

**But what is his real story?**

# Shakuni

Beads of sweat dripped into Shakuni's eyes. He felt as though people were boring holes in his back with incriminating glances, like white hot rods. This was the moment he had lived for, waited for, hungered for, all his life. Tainting the joy of his victory, however, was a deep, unsettling, and unfamiliar emotion. How could this be a victory if it made him feel so...guilty? Was this really what he wanted? Was it worth it to achieve his dreams...like this?

✶✶✶✶✶✶✶✶✶✶✶

The princess of Gandhara, Gandhari, was known as one of the bravest, smartest, and most beautiful women in all of the rose apple continent of Jambudvipa. She was the apple of her parents' eyes and the beloved of all the kingdom. She spent her days with her brother Shakuni, their bright smiles and happy faces bringing joy to the kingdom. She loved watching him perfect his natural attraction to and skill at dice. However, she had only one flaw: she was under the influence of a horrible curse, one that could disfigure her flawless reputation and destroy all her hopes of ever having a happy life. She had been cursed to become the bringer of Yama to her husband, the cause of his downfall, the harbinger of his death. To evade the effects of this one vice among their daughter's thousand virtues, as infinite as the ocean of milk Vishnu sleeps on, her parents decided to marry her off to a goat, and then sacrifice it, thus fulfilling the prophecy without utterly and completely undoing her future.

Having completed this task in secrecy, as advised by Veda Vyasa, the great ascetic and ancestor of the Kuru dynasty, her father, Subala, turned his attention to the many requests for marital alliances for Gandhari.

When he learned that the Kuru prince, Dhritarashtra, was one of her suitors, he felt bittersweet. Marrying Gandhari to Dhritarashtra would mean a great alliance with the Kurus and a good family. On the other hand, her husband Dhritarashtra being blind, Gandhari would forever be ridiculed. Finally, the allure of the alliance was too much and he agreed.

After a grand marriage, Gandhari was bid goodbye by a heavy-hearted Shakuni.

A few years passed and, eventually, Bhishma, the patriarch of the Kuru household, found out about Gandhari's secret. Enraged that a widow had entered the noble house of Kuru, he imprisoned her father Subala and all his hundred sons, including Shakuni. Every day, a fist of rice would be pushed through the door. Subala realised that only one person can survive on this much food and should be the one to avenge all of them. Shakuni was chosen to be that one.

With his dying breath, Subala broke his dear son's leg to forever remind him of the reason he was alive and told him to carve dice out of his finger bones.

*"With your skill and my thirst for vengeance, the dice will obey your every thought and give you...a gift. Use it wisely to fulfil your debt to those who are the reason for your survival, those to whom you are indebted."*

With that, Subala died. After his death, Shakuni was brought to Hastinapura after much pleading on Gandhari's part.

Many, many, many years later, Duryodhana was born. Rather than reducing or numbing the pain, time had allowed Shakuni's pain and thirst for vengeance to fester in him, leaving him more determined than ever to destroy the Kurus.

At Duryodhana's birth, several bad omens such as dogs howling were witnessed. At this, Shakuni gave a sly smile; here were the means through which he would achieve vengeance and avenge his family.

As Duryodhana grew up, his natural jealousy of the Pandavas was noticed and encouraged by Shakuni. Against Dhritarashtra's will, Vidura, the paternal uncle of both Pandavas and Kauravas, convinced him to give Khandavaprastha, a forested fertile region of Hastinapura to the Pandavas . Upon Krishna's advice, they converted it into Indraprastha. The Pandavas invited Duryodhana to their Rajasuya yagna. Even though they had benevolent intentions, Shakuni convinced Duryodhana that they were secretly malevolent. Duryodhana, ready to mock the Pandavas and full of contempt, went to Indraprastha and got the shock of a lifetime at the intricate Palace of Illusions. He was tricked by a pond so crystal clear he mistook it for a glass floor and fell into it. A watching Draupadi laughed and insulted him.

*"Look Sairandhri* ! The blind son of a blind king!"*

He returned to Hastinapura and was greeted by Shakuni, delighted to see that his rage and hatred had multiplied by a hundredfold. He decided that now was the right time to use his father's blessing...or was it more of a curse?

He said to Duryodhana:

*"O valiant prince! O son of Dhritarashtra! O heir to the noble throne of Hastinapura! O illustrious harbinger of righteousness! O descendant of Puru! O Indra on Earth! O king of kings, I have a plan to overthrow your evil, ill-omened cousins. I have a plan to make you the sole monarch of Bharatvarsha, the greatest ruler the world has ever seen!"*

**Sairandhri - A female attendant employed by royals.*

*"OK, OK! Just tell me the plan- enough with the flattery."*

At this, Shakuni grimaced in despair and quickly covered it up with a devoted smile.

*"Of course, of course! Anything your lordship states. I have a special pair of dice. They will always obey me, no matter what. They are among my most prized possessions, a gift from my late father."*

*"So?"*

*"Yudishtira may be seen as very virtuous and respectable and all, but he has one vice."*

*"What?"*

Duryodhana was now visibly excited and intrigued.

*"He cannot resist or refuse an invitation to a game of dice."*

As he said this, a smile of comprehension and excitement passed over Duryodhana's face.

They had a special hall built for the purpose and invited the Pandavas to a game of dice. By noon, the guests had arrived.

*"Ah! Finally! Shall we begin?"*

*"Hmmm! Duryodhana, I didn't notice this hall last time I was here."*

*"Oh no, this hall is built specifically for you my dear cousins. Now, I assume Yudishtira will be playing for the Pandavas?"*

*"Yes, and you for the Kauravas?"*

*"No, no, my maternal uncle Shakuni will be delighted to play you."*

At this, the game of dice began. Yudishtira, as predicted, lost everything.

*"Now I have lost everything! I'm done with this Ill-fated game," cried Yudishtira.*

*"No, no, how about one final wager? You still have Draupadi."*

The entire court gasped at this vulgar suggestion. However, Yudishtira staked Draupadi…and lost!

*"Now, bring in Draupadi,"* thundered Shakuni.

The entire court watched in shame as Draupadi was brought in, dragged by the hair.

*"Ah, now here are the valiant Pandavas and their grand queen Draupadi! Now, you all are our slaves. Uncle, get my brother Dushasana to rid them of their grand finery, not suited to a servant's status."*

The Pandavas threw off their clothes and jewellery before Dushasana could touch them and gasped at an order from Duryodhana.

*"Her too."*

What! Humiliate the greatest queen who has ever lived in a way unimaginable to any woman? Disrobe her? Destroy her honour and position? The court watched with bated breath as Dushasana pulled off her sari…and found another underneath! Draupadi had been saved by an intervention of the divine!

Dhritarashtra had finally seen sense.

*"Now! Stop with this madness. Daughter-in-law, I grant you three boons in exchange for your troubles."*

She immediately held on to his words.

*"Firstly, let Yudishtira be freed, secondly, let everything he lost be returned to him."*

*"Done and done. Now, how about something for yourself?"*

*"My husbands' debts are fulfilled. That is all."*

Shakuni said in desperation,

*"Oho! Are the Pandavas saved by...their strength, their courage, their wit, their beauty, their knowledge? No no...these once great rulers are saved by their queen! If you have any honour left, I offer you one last wager. The winner gets everything, the loser is exiled for twelve years and spends a year incognito. If discovered, they must repeat the thirteen years."*

Unable to bear this insult, Yudishtira agreed. He played.

And lost.

At the end of the exile, when they came back for their kingdom, Shakuni goaded Duryodhana into refusing them. This led to the great war of Kurukshetra.

✶✶✶✶✶✶✶✶✶✶✶

Krishna's conch sounded to herald the beginning of the war and Shakuni came out of his reverie.

As he foretold, on the eleventh day of the war, Shakuni tried to lead his armies against Arjuna but was brutally defeated due to Arjuna's archery skills. After the death of Shalya, the commander, Shakuni realised that Yudishtira, Bhima, and Arjuna were leading the army and the rear flanks were left unprotected. He rallied the Gandhara army and ambushed the Pandavas from behind, against the rules of righteous war. Yudishtira sent Nakula and Sahadeva to hold off Shakuni. A great fight ensued, during the end of which, the youngest Pandava, Sahadeva, managed to strike him down and kill him.

As he breathed his last, he realised, too late, that the destruction of the Kuru household wasn't his dream; it was his father's. He would die, having lived a meaningless life and having destroyed crores more.

And thus, innocent brotherly love and family pride led an illustrious boy astray; turned him into the most hated character; turned a boy with the potential to be the king of kings into... an evil sidekick, a manipulator. Shakuni's story teaches us the importance of never letting life shake your morals.

## Many say...

"She was weak and submissive."

"She paid no heed to her children's callousness."

"She was Dhritarashtra's shadow."

## But what is her real story?

# Gandhari

The traditional red silk, gold embroidered sari, and shining gold jewellery of the maiden signified her status as a bride. The richness of said attire showed that she was of, and had been married into, a royal family. She was Gandhari, princess of Gandhara, daughter of King Subala and Queen Sudharmaa, sister of Shakuni and now wife of Dhritarashtra, the blind king of Hastinapur.

As she climbed onto the palanquin, she glanced back at her maternal home, aware she was leaving behind the place that shaped her, that contained all the people she loved, to live somewhere else with a man she didn't even know, and a lone tear ran down her long, slender nose, the only sign of emotion she showed.

She settled herself onto her feather pillows and got ready for the one-and-a-half-day-long journey to Kuru, her new home. Peeking through the organza curtains at the snow-capped peaks of Gandhara, its former princess prepared to replace them with the green-blanketed hills of Kurukshetra.

A few years earlier, on a hot, sunny day in the mountainous kingdom of Gandhara, a fine young man ran through the pillared, red sandstone corridors of a palace, in hot pursuit of a bonny young girl who bore an uncanny remembrance to him, her long, beautiful, and silky hair streaming behind her. A Sairandhri chased the pair, stopping to catch her breath.

*"Oh, princess Gandhari! If you continue running like that, your hair will become terribly knotted."*

Just then, the queen happened to arrive at the same corridor.

*"Oh! Lakshmi, what happened?"*

*"Your Highness, the princess is refusing to let her hair be braided."*

Later, the queen spoke to the king.

*"Seeing her laugh and run is such a joy. Little does she know about the black cloud she was born with."*

At this, the queen broke down.

*"It is all going to be okay."*

*"No, it's not! Her first husband is to die soon after her marriage. I am worried for her future and ours. We are a small kingdom. If her husband's family finds out about her curse after it has come to pass, I...I can't even imagine what they would do to her. And us!"*

Gandhari heard everything as she eavesdropped through the keyhole. At this, she let out a choked sob and ran to her bedchamber. Hearing the sound of running feet, her parents ran out the door, trying to catch up with her as she ran. Ripping off her ornaments, she threw herself onto her bed and cried into her pillow. Her parents followed her. Her father helplessly watched as mother and child sobbed together.

Comforting them, he said,

*"Everything will be alright. Let's...let's just calm down and consult Bhagavan Veda Vyasa. He is our greatest and wisest advisor."*

✶✶✶✶✶✶✶✶✶✶✶

Gandhari waited at the palace gate at sunset, anxiously looking out for her parents. As the royal sentries serenaded their return, her eyes widened in apprehension. What news had they brought? She took deep breaths to steady herself, hoping, praying, that the words to be uttered by her father would provide her hope for a happy life.

*"My dear! You did not have to stand here waiting! How long have you been here?"*

*"Um…uh...ever since you left?"*

*"But we left at sunrise!"*

*"I know, I know. But enough of that father, tell me, what is to become of my fate?"*

*"My dear, keep hope. There is an ancient ritual that will relieve you of your curse and let you live a long and happy life…at your marital home. "*

*"What! You plan to doom an innocent man!"*

*"No, no, you would be married to a goat…."*

*"And then you would kill the goat! That is a truly ingenious solution! But what would people think?"*

*"You always were a sharp girl. And as for the people, this ritual would be performed in secret. But know, my child, that this is a very common practice. We are only being secretive due to the Kuru's infamous short temper. They have asked for your hand for their Prince and we don't want anything to jeopardise the situation."*

On the fateful day, Gandhari was woken up early in the morning and led to a remote clearing in the forest, where she was married to the goat and it was subsequently beheaded. A messenger was then sent to Kurukshetra, accepting the marriage offer.

✶✶✶✶✶✶✶✶✶✶✶

Gandhari mustered up her courage and composed her face into one of regal elegance as she got down from the palanquin, preparing to meet her grandmother-in-law, Satyavathi, the matriarch of the Kuru household.

She walked into the ornate palace of Kurukshetra, golden and gem-studded like a goblet. Recollecting all she had learned about poise and grace from her mother, she set forward with a light step, gently swaying hips and a sweet smile gracing her lips, a flower offering to goddess Durga in hand.

She entered the courtroom, pageboys heralding her. She was received with a gracious smile from Satyavathi, but Gandhari couldn't help noticing that the smile never reached her eyes.

She was then guided to her chambers to get some rest before her wedding the next day.

✶✶✶✶✶✶✶✶✶✶✶

That night, as she lay in the soft feather bed, so much more extravagant than her own, yet not as comfortable, she heard a mirthful voice.

*"Wedding worries? You know, insomnia is quite common at this juncture."*

*"Kunti, I now desire a son who is fit to be the warrior of warriors! Call upon Devendra Indra."*

*"As you wish, my lord."*

After Arjuna was born from Indra, Kunti was called upon one last time.

*"I do not desire that the young and beautiful Madri remain childless on account of my curse. Teach her this mantra."*

*"As you wish, my lord."*

Madri called upon the Ashwini Kumaras and bore them twins: Nakula and Sahadeva.

Together, the three raised their kids in peace and Pandu was happy for a few years.

✶✶✶✶✶✶✶✶✶✶✶

Gandhari was in the garden, holding baby Duryodhana and playing with him when a maid was sent to call her urgently to court.

*"Now?"*

*"Yes, my queen. And the king says to hurry."*

She dropped off baby Duryodhana with the nurses and ran to court. It must be something serious, as she hadn't been called to court since her sons had been born. She entered to find a panting messenger and a livid Dhritarashtra.

*"My queen! This messenger is from Pandu's wife, Kunti. And he claims that- I'll let him say it."*

*"My liege, crown prince Pandu died under the influence of sage Kindama's curse. His younger wife, Madri, jumped onto his funeral pyre, leaving behind her twins, Nakula and Sahadeva, and Kunti with her three sons, Yudishtira, Bhima, and Arjuna. They are on their way to the palace and will arrive tomorrow. "*

At that moment, even though Gandhari's eyes were covered, she felt a strong, unexplained aura emerging from her husband.

✶✶✶✶✶✶✶✶✶✶✶

*"Urgh! Not again!"*

The princes had been playing their favourite game: climb the tree. As usual, Bhima had used his strength and shaken the trees so hard, the Kauravas fell like mangoes, with the mangoes.

This time, he had gone one step further and chased the Kauravas all around the palace and then forced them to gather, peel, cut, and feed him the mangoes.

Burning with rage, the Kauravas swore to have revenge. Duryodhana fed Bhima poisoned sweets, bound his legs, and threw him into the river. A satisfied Duryodhana headed back to the palace and feigned ignorance when his disappearance was noticed. A frantic search ensued, the result of which, of course, resulted in more panic as he was nowhere to be found.

In the meantime, Bhima sank all the way to Nagaloka where the snakes bit him.

Their poison counteracted the poison from the sweets and Bhima was instantly revived and started killing all the snakes trying to kill him. Eventually, the king of snakes and his advisors rushed to the scene where they begged him to stop.

*"And why should I trust you or have mercy on you? You were about to kill me!"*

Suddenly, Vasuki, an advisor to the snake king, recognised him.

*"No! Stop! He was part of my human family!"*

At this, the Nagas thanked Bhima and fed him a drink that gave him the strength of a thousand elephants with every mouthful. He had eight mouthfuls of it and was grandly escorted back to the surface.

By this time, two weeks had passed since Bhima's disappearance and everyone was preparing for his last rites. Just when they were about to begin, Bhima stormed into the hall and pointed an accusing finger at Duryodhana.

When he returned, the anxious knot that had tightened in Gandhari's chest and seemed to be squeezing the life out of her, loosened.

Bhima explained what Duryodhana had done to him and forced him to publicly apologise. He then calmed down and consoled his mother and brothers. Soon, he saw the huge amount of ingredients arranged to prepare the feast and felt bad it would be wasted. He then used his cooking expertise to make a dish out of it called aviyal.

When Bhima accused Duryodhana and the latter admitted to his crime, Gandhari's face turned deathly pale. Later, in her chambers, she raged at him.

*"How could you? He is your cousin! How could you make an attempt on his life over some petty, childish fight? I expected better of you! What kind of an example are you setting for your siblings?"*

At this, Duryodhana burst into crocodile tears. His mother quickly calmed down and comforted him. This occurred many, many times. Each time, he went unpunished. That was a choice she would pay for dearly.

* * * * * * * * * * *

"*My queen, Gandhari."*

*"Vidura."*

*"Duryodhana's latest plot against his cousins, the erstwhile Pandavas, is simply too much. Could you not punish him or speak to him, make him see reason?*

*"I know, I know, but Duryodhana is my firstborn! I love him more than anything in the world. But, I too desire the safety and happiness of the sons of my brother-in-law. Hmmmm."*

With this, she paused, pondering the issue. Suddenly, she got it!

*"Brother Vidura, would it help if we gave the Pandavas their own palace?"*

*"What a brainwave! That would solve all our problems! I will suggest this excellent course of action to my brother."*

✶✶✶✶✶✶✶✶✶✶✶

Gandhari's intention to give the Pandavas their own palace was noble but the way her son and husband were involved in building a palace in Varanavata for them made her feel uneasy. Many times she felt she should speak up about it but now, it was too late. The palace was ready and the Pandavas began to reside in it.

One day, her worst suspicions came true with shocking news.

She heard that the Pandavas, along with their elderly mother Kunti, had died in the fire at Varanavata! Upon hearing this, Gandhari fell extremely ill. Eventually, after all the vaidyas had failed, in desperation, they called in Veda Vyasa. When Veda Vyasa entered, a sense of calm spread through the room and Gandhari felt better. He immediately knew the cause of her illness and whispered something in her ear. Immediately, Gandhari's face lit up and she looked almost back to normal. She got out of bed, did a namaskara to him and thanked him profusely.

Everyone speculated as to what he might have whispered, but only she knew the truth.

*"The Pandavas survived. Vidura helped them. Thank him."*

✶✶✶✶✶✶✶✶✶✶✶

Throughout the years until the Pandavas won Draupadi, while Dhritarashtra mourned and Duryodhana rejoiced, Gandhari and Vidura were the only ones who knew the truth. During these years, she rewarded Vidura for the smallest of services and praised him. She chastised Duryodhana for making simple mistakes, all the while carrying Panadava's survival as a sort of emblem of hope within her.

When the Pandavas arrived in Hastinapura with their beautiful wife Draupadi and asked for their share of the kingdom, Gandhari sensed that trouble was brewing. She suggested to Duryodhana that the Pandavas get the portion of Kurukshetra called Khandavaprastha, leaving Hastinapura for Duryodhana. He agreed and for some time everything was fine. She breathed a sigh of relief, believing war to be averted. Little did she know, this was but the calm before the storm.

When the Pandavas invited Duryodhana to see Indraprastha, Gandhari begged him not to go, telling him it was a trap. And indeed it was! He returned, humiliated and dejected. Plotting with Gandhari's brother, Shakuni, Duryodhana arranged for the fatal dice game that would seal the fate of the Kauravas.

During the game of dice, as Gandhari listened to Draupadi's screams while being disrobed by Gandhari's own son, her face burned with shame. When Draupadi was saved through divine intervention, Gandhari forced Dhritarashtra to reverse everything and relaxed when everything was returned to normal. When Shakuni incited them to play one more round, Gandhari had to use all her self control to not give him a piece of her mind. She was among the few truly dismayed about the turn of events.

Hearing the curses uttered by Bhima and Draupadi, Gandhari felt a sense of foreboding. Once she recovered, she too slept on the floor, thinking of their discomfort, feeling guilty as though she was responsible for it.

Thirteen years later, when news came that the Pandavas had been located at and had defeated the Kauravas at Matsya, Gandhari was simultaneously thrilled and saddened. The fact that the Pandavas had returned meant that they had survived the arduous exile, but Gandhari was scared of what would happen if the Kauravas didn't keep their promise.

When the Pandavas came for their share of the kingdom, and, as predicted, were refused by the Kauravas, Gandhari had half a mind to shout at her sons, correct them, save them before it was too late. However, hearing her son Duryodhana proclaiming he would never even give up a needlepoint of land to the Pandavas made her voice die in her throat.

A few days later, when Krishna Vasudeva came as the last peace mediator and suggested that the Kauravas give up five villages to the Pandavas, Gandhari prayed and hoped that the impossible would happen and the inevitable wouldn't; that Duryodhana would agree. However, hearing Duryodhana tell the guards to arrest Krishna silenced her once again.

For the next few days, Gandhari's heart threw up forbidden emotions. She wasn't supposed to feel love for the sworn enemies of her husband and son! But she did. And while you can't control your heart, you can control your actions. So, Gandhari threw herself into her kingdom and her duties preparing rations for the war.

✶✶✶✶✶✶✶✶✶✶✶

Gandhari awoke with a start. She knew someone was in the room, and she sensed who it was too.

*"Bhagavan Veda Vyasa."*

*"Yes, it is me. You know, I often think fate must have a sense of humour! I seem to have appeared before you several times; each time, it was before or after a critical moment in your life."*

*"But didn't you choose to come here? What does fate have to do with it?"*

*"Ah, you have asked the very question I was sent to you to answer. You see, there are those primordial forces which have designed this wondrous system: Karma. Every action and reaction is both preordained... and not."*

*"I don't understand. It is preordained and not?"*

*"My child, even though you may think you are yourself performing actions, these actions are being prompted by situations prompted by previous actions. It is this curious cycle we live in, making mistakes, realising that we must live our lives pure, dying, and making more mistakes!"*

*"But..."*

*"Why am I telling you this? I am trying to brace you for the future. I am trying to prevent you from making a few fatal mistakes. But this is again preordained. Just like everything in life. Remember, nothing is forever and you shape your future through your actions. You have gained enormous powers through your chastity over the years. Do not misuse them."*

✶✶✶✶✶✶✶✶✶✶✶

*"May the most righteous win."*

Her hundred sons had come to get her blessings before the war began. She knew that her duty as her mother was to wish them victory, but she simply couldn't as everything Gandhari said came true, as she only spoke the truth. She didn't know who would win, only that the most righteous would win.

*"Ah! How I wish I could see this!"*

She sighed. Dhritarashtra had started on one of his rants again. Only this time, someone came forward to help him.

*"Would you like to have sight of this particular war?"*

*"Bhagavan Vyasa. No, I am not such a bloodthirsty man. I do not wish to see death with my own eyes. However, I wish I could know what would happen on the battlefield,"* said Dhritarashtra.

Veda Vyasa hesitated for a moment and then turned to Dhritarashtra's royal advisor, Sanjay.

*"May you have divine sight for this war. You will be able to see everything that goes on in the battlefield from here and will have the acute power of narrating these events without bias."*

✶✶✶✶✶✶✶✶✶✶✶

Even though she had known subconsciously what would happen for a long time, Gandhari still couldn't believe it. She was numb with disbelief, sunk deep in grief. Her sons...her beautiful sons...all were dead except her eldest, prince of her heart. She now felt a love for him that was protective and fierce, resembling but wholly overpowering the love she had felt for him the day he was born. She had lived her whole life righteously, biding by the rules, trying to be perfect at every point, but this was it. This was her breaking point. She could NOT lose her last son Duryodhana.

When he came to take Gandhari's blessings for the final battle against Bhima, she told him.

*"I have accumulated immense power through my chastity and devotion. Take a bath in the Ganga and come to me like you were the day you were born. I will make you invincible."*

✶✶✶✶✶✶✶✶✶✶✶

As Gandhari removed her blindfold for the first time since her marriage, she took a moment to take in all the colours. It was too much for her, too bright! But then, her eyes passed over his tousled hair, his shining eyes, his chiselled chin, his powerful arms, and then...a banana leaf. Anger erupted inside Gandhari , mixed with sadness. Her powers would make every area of her son she saw, as strong as a diamond. But now...he was doomed. However, Gandhari tied back her blindfold and put on an impassive face, hoping what was about to happen wouldn't happen after all.

As she heard the vivid description from Sanjay, she covered her ears and wrung her head trying not to listen.

*"Duryodhana has the upper hand in the battle right now. However, Bhima, close to giving up, glances at Krishna, who slaps his thighs, reminding Bhima of his vow. Bhima raises his mace and breaks Duryodhana's thighs. The war is over."*

Coming out of his trance, Sanjay tried to console the inconsolable couple. While Dhritarashtra was quite overcome and had fainted, Gandhari sat straight and stiff, the refusal to believe radiating from her. She had done everything for her son; why hadn't she done better? Maybe if she had been stricter..?

*"Don't. It's not your fault."*

*"Bhagavan Veda Vyasa."*

*"I warned you before the war. This is not your fault. Your sons brought this upon themselves."*

Suddenly, a herald announced the return of the victors, the Pandavas. Seeing them, her heart swelled with an insidious mixture of anger and love.

When Dhritarashtra tried to crush Bhima to death but ended up crushing an iron statue, she seethed with rage. While her husband seemed to have gotten over his anger and was apologising, as usual, she was going through more. Yudishtira came to take her blessings but her fiery gaze would have killed him too, had Krishna not pulled him away. But this was it. She was done. She lashed out at Krishna, showing all her anger and pain and sorrow on him.

*"You! You are the reason I am childless. The reason my Duryodhana is dead. The cause of my sorrow. Weren't they both your cousins? But still, you always favoured the Pandavas. I curse you! May your clan destroy each other as mine did!"*

* * * * * * * * * * *

It had been sixteen years since her sons had died. Gandhari had, surprisingly enough, gotten over her anger. She had come to realise (or so she thought) the true meaning of Bhagavan Veda Vyasa's words. She had brought up her great grandson Parikshit. She had reconciled with the Pandavas. It was time to leave. When she suggested this to her husband, who had gotten increasingly bitter over the years, isolating himself further, he pounced on the idea as a starved animal does on food. Kunti, Vidura and Sanjay decided to accompany them. The Pandavas helped set up their hut. They asked for Gandhari's blessings, after Kunti and they both blessed the Pandavas wholeheartedly.

In the forest, Dhrithrashtra persuaded Gandhari to remove her blindfold. She had seen him so many years ago on the day of her wedding and now after building a life together, she was seeing her husband again. She could barely recognize him. Rushing to check her own reflection, she was surprised at the toll age had taken on both of them.

One day, there was a forest fire. Holding Kunti's hand, Gandhari walked into it.

In those few seconds before death, she found herself transported into a nether world. There, she saw Him. Lord Vishnu, lying on his snake the Adi-Ananta-Sesha. Seeing his eternal form, she finally understood the full meaning of Karma, before dying peacefully with an enlightened smile on her face.

And thus, an august maiden renowned for her beauty and intelligence fell prey to relentless power struggles. Gandhari's story teaches us the dangers of mistaken humility.

**Many say....**

"He was biased and partial."

"He was unfit to be king."

"His birth was an accident."

**What was his true story?**

# Vidura

A man with the bearing of a king but in commoner's attire hurried along the corridor, his eyes spinning, ears ringing with what he had just heard. He knew of the petty rivalry between the Pandava and Kaurava cousins, but didn't know Duryodhana would go this far. Yet, after willing to underhandedly kill his cousins, Duryodhana still had the audacity to proclaim himself a worthy ruler!

Those poor Pandava boys! They came to this palace seeking comfort, solace and a home, and instead got a house filled with political intrigue and ulterior motives. If he didn't act quickly, the only surviving descendants of his brother Pandu would be gone! No, he couldn't let them die that way.

That night, he retired early saying he was feeling unwell, and, when everyone was asleep, met...an ally. He had this man warn the Pandavas that the palace they believed was a loving gift from their uncle was really a death trap. He had the man take materials and a plan to escape.

Whatever happened, even if he had to give up his life for it, he could not let this adharmic murder occur.

* * * * * * * * * * * *

The leaves of the peepal tree moved with the wind. A wiry ascetic with a serene smile meditated under it. As he was in a trance, he didn't notice when two thieves crept into his ashrama. Moments later, a few guards emerged and asked the sage if he had seen the thieves.

*"Greetings, sage Mandavya. Have you seen anyone around here?"*

He didn't reply, so the guards searched the ashrama. They found them, and, as the sage hadn't given them that information, they assumed he was helping the thieves and took him to the king. The king was enraged and decreed that they must be impaled by a thousand nails without proper investigation. The two thieves died but sage Mandavya remained alive through his yogic powers. Eventually, the guards informed the king of this. Horrified, he apologised and called the best physicians in the land to remove the nails. They were able to remove all but one. The kind sage blessed the king and went on his way.

A few years later, the nail was causing him immense pain. So, he went to the god of death, Yama himself, to ask the reason for his suffering.

*"Oh great sage, in your previous life, when you were a little boy, you enjoyed putting twigs into butterflies bodies and watching them die. This is your punishment."*

At this, Mandavya was enraged.

*"Oh Yama, you claim to be so wise, yet I am suffering for an adolescent mistake. I curse you! You shall be born on Earth as a human and will be the sole voice of reason as insanity occurs around you. Further, from now on, any mistakes committed before a child's twelfth birthday will be the parents' Karma."*

*"I understand. From now on, for this great service to the world, you will be called Animandavya. Ani means a small nail, so your pain will be remembered forever."*

Satyavathi was enraged. Three disappointments in a row! The first heir to her kingdom, Dhritarashtra, was born blind. The second, Pandu, an invalid. And now, when the perfect heir had finally been born, he wasn't even of royal blood! His mother was a handmaiden!

Named Vidura, the cherubic little boy lay in the royal cradle, sleeping peacefully. She wanted to scream! This was surely the end. There was no way her kingdom would survive now! She sent the baby away. Only upon the pleading of her daughter-in-law did she grudgingly consent to the child being raised with her grandsons.

Growing up, Vidura's life wasn't easy. He was constantly reminded that he was second-class to his brothers and would never even be in line for the throne. However, he soon won everyone over with his wit. He was an unusual child, sharp and very quick, an excellent student. He learned all there is to know about the shastras and kingship and begged his brother, Dhritarashtra to let him be his royal advisor.

When Pandu left for the forest, Vidura suddenly took on a much more important role, being the only person Dhritarashtra trusted. Every time there was an open display of enmity between the cousins, he tried to advocate for the Pandavas, fighting to get them an equal status with their cousins. He took a special liking to Yudishtira, the uniquely perceptive boy being mistreated, reminding him of himself. Vidura was the only father figure the Pandavas ever knew. He played and wrestled with the Pandavas, providing support to Kunti as she braved the wilderness of being a widowed single mother.

When Bhima was nearly killed by Duryodhana, Vidura had half a mind to lash out. However, knowing his brother, Vidura took a different approach.

After consulting Gandhari, he suggested they build a different palace for the Pandavas. When he found out they were actually under threat of murder, Vidura arranged for their escape. All the years they were in the forest, he too slept on the floor, thinking of their discomfort. He ate only the simplest of foods, wore the simplest of clothes, and refused to take part in any activities of any sort. He even built a hut for himself a little way away from the palace and lived there for the ten years when the Pandavas were in hiding.

Most people who knew him thought he was in mourning for the Pandavas and left him alone. Only Duryodhana disturbed him.

*"Of course, you have always loved them more! Although, what is there to love? They aren't even that special!"*

*"Don't... don't say that. I love you all equally."*

At this, Duryodhana rolled his eyes and walked off, still feeling that small pinch of jealousy every time Vidura declined his offers to go to any festivals etc. This was only the beginning of the slights he would face from Duryodhana.

* * * * * * * * * * * *

The Pandavas entered the court dressed in their finery, leading their beautiful queen, Draupadi, behind them. Vidura had heard tales of her unique comeliness, but he was startled when he looked into her eyes. There was something, a sense of infinitesimal power that radiated from her that made Vidura bow his head as she walked past.

The Pandavas were greeted by a sense of such happiness from Duryodhana that it was quite obvious it was fake. The only people with genuine joy in the room, Vidura observed, were the commoners who had come to see their beloved princes.

When Yudishtira came to him for his blessings, Vidura wholeheartedly blessed him, lifted him up, and locked him in a tight embrace. He kissed his forehead and proceeded to greet the rest for the brothers with the same enthusiasm. Later, he invited them all back to his hut for lunch. Declining the offer of a luxurious lunch at the palace, they followed Vidura to his hut to help with the preparation of a meal filled with delightful banter and heartfelt memories.

✶✶✶✶✶✶✶✶✶✶✶

*"No! Don't! Please! Grand-uncle Bhishma! Mother Gandhari! Uncle Vidura!"*

Draupadi's screams tore through Vidura's heart. The Pandavas had just played a horrid round of dice and bet and lost Draupadi.

Oh that poor, poor child! She was once queen of such a status that even Sachi, the queen of the heavens, was said to be jealous of her. Now, she was in the royal court, being subjected to humiliation even the most peasant women of Hastinapura didn't face! And he was powerless. Again. When the Pandavas had been subjected to humiliation all their childhood, he was powerless. When they had been given the inferior part for the kingdom, Khandavaprastha, he was powerless. Now, he was powerless even to save the dignity of Draupadi, the most prized queen in the land. There was only one thing that had worked then, and it would work now.

He closed his eyes and began chanting the name of Vishnu, the Eternal Protector. Then, as though by a miracle, she was saved! As she was being disrobed, Panchali's sari seemed never-ending! Seeing this as an opportunity, he advised Dhritarashtra to intervene before he and his children were cursed. And so it was. Draupadi was given three boons with which she retrieved everything her husbands had lost. All was well...for that moment.

Desperate, Shakuni, shouted out.

*"What, you need your wife to save you, huh? Now, if you are a real man, come and play another round of dice! Winner takes all. Losers have to spend twelve years in exile and one year incognito before being able to reclaim their kingdom. If found they have to repeat all thirteen years again."*

At that moment, Vidura knew. He knew the answer before it left Yudhishtira's lips. He knew the future before it occurred. And most importantly, he knew there was nothing he could do to stop it. A faint memory resurfaced; him warning Yudishtira.

*"Your pride will be your downfall."*

✶✶✶✶✶✶✶✶✶✶✶✶

After all his efforts, it had come to this.

The court was almost in session. Yet, the noisy hubbub that usually filled the atmosphere was absent, for they awaited a special guest. Before he saw him, he felt his presence. The sound of a sweetly played flute reaching his ears. Then, he saw him. The infinite blue skin, the yellow silk, the peacock feather in his hair. A sense of calm washed over him.

However, Krishna's presence only seemed to agitate Duryodhana.

*"Yes. You...uh...came."*

*"Now, is that a way to greet your cousin?!"*

*"No. Uh..."*

*"I came as a mediator of peace from the Pandavas."*

*"Yes."*

*"They request you to return their Indraprastha to them."*

*"No. Never!"*

*"Then, at least give them five villages."*

*"Go back, go back to your precious Pandavas and tell them, I will never give them even a needlepoint of MY kingdom! Guards! Arrest him!"*

In that moment, a palpable energy filled the air. Krishna transformed into...into something terrifying and beautiful at the same time. In his eyes, Vidura saw the heavens, the earth, himself staring at his eyes. And then...the moment ended.

Krishna was himself again. Duryodhana, realising his mistake, offered him dinner, which he politely declined. Instead, to his great surprise, Krishna requested to dine at Vidura's house!

Vidura cooked him a meal of love and affection and then took him for a horse ride. While riding he asked Krishna many questions about the universe which the latter cryptically answered.

*"What is Karma?"*

*"Karma is the concept of action and reaction, in which the fruit of our actions, whether good or bad, always comes back to us."*

*"What did I ever do to deserve this life, in which no one ever listens to me and I am downgraded based on my birth?"*

*"Everyone has done something or the other to deserve their situations. Your life is not your fault, but your past birth's consequences. However, always remember, you are responsible for your next situation, so always do good and abide by Dharma. These situations can easily be braved through hard work and belief in the divine."*

That night, as Vidura slept on the ground, he visualised Krishna's serene face and pondered at the answers he had given him, before falling asleep while gazing at the pearly surface of the moon.

✶✶✶✶✶✶✶✶✶✶✶

Even after all these years, Vidura found it simply impossible that his Yudishtira, whom he had raised, had uttered a lie during the Kurukshetra war. All his life, Yudishtira had been so truthful even his chariot floated four inches off the ground. Now, he was equal to other men. It didn't matter that they won the war, it mattered they had killed a man through adharmic ways. His Yudishtira!

That's why, when Kunti announced that she, along with Gandhari, Sanjay and Dhritarashtra were planning to retire to the forest, he decided to accompany them.

✶✶✶✶✶✶✶✶✶✶✶

One day, a thin, bony old man lay on his hard charpoy, staring at the ceiling of his mud hut. He looked to his left and saw two old women, both with serene smiles on their faces, blissfully sleeping on a similar cot. To his immediate right lay a man so thin his ribs were seen through the thin, old saree spread on him. Even in sleep, Dhritarashtra's fiery temper, so close to the surface nowadays, was seen.

He couldn't feign sleep any longer. It had been days since he had slept as the others did, from sunset to dawn.

Vidura got out of bed and went to the river for his early morning rituals. As he stared at his reflection in the water, he had an epiphany.

What was he doing here? He had grown up alone. He had lived his life alone among an overflowing household. Even now, in the serenity of the forest, he was alone! Except he wasn't. All his life, in his darkest moments, amid his greatest triumphs, one person had stuck by him. That being was...

Krishna.

He knew what he had to do. He went to the place. His secret place. The temple.

As he walked to the temple, the secret Krishna shrine where he meditated every evening, he realised,

*"Kanha is everywhere! Wherever I am, Krishna's love will reach me."*

He stood in the yogic posture Vrikshasana and slowly started chanting.

*"Hare Rama, Hare Rama, Rama Rama, Hare Hare!*
*Hare Krishna, Hare Krishna, Krishna Krishna, Hare Hare!"*

As his senses took leave of him one by one, the last thing he experienced on Earth was the sound of Yudishtira's voice...and a vision.

In it, he saw everything. His past life, the reason for his birth, the future. Then, he realised that his knowledge couldn't go to waste. He was Yama. He didn't have the luxury of dying, he was the one who aided death! No, he must leave for his world, Yamaloka, in another way.

✶✶✶✶✶✶✶✶✶✶✶

One day, after not seeing Vidura for long, Dhritarashtra got worried and called Yudishtira. After a vigorous search, they found him, or rather what remained of him, in the forest.

He had not eaten for many months now. He was standing in a yogic posture, his empty husk of a body looking fragile, his skin transparent. As they approached him, a bolt of light shot out of his head and into Yudishtira, merging their souls. As this happened, his body crumbled and he became one with Prithvi Mata, where he had come from.

At that moment, Yudishtira smiled. He now understood. The anguish on his face now replaced with serenity, the people around him were confused. Bhima and Kunti wiped their eyes and asked him what happened.

*"Vidura...was an incarnation of the divine. A deva born as human. As such, he can never die, for how could one who had drunk Amrita succumb to the petty fatality of death? But more than anything, this is a sign. A sign for us to begin our final journey. Come."*

*"But what was the bolt of light?"*

*"He has given me his knowledge so his great learnings don't go to waste. We are now one. Father and son united. Come, we must prepare for the final journey."*

And thus, the exalted one who came from the heavens returned to the heavens.

Vidura embodies the theme of the Mahabharata and all of mankind: balance.

The balance between good and evil, the balance between right and wrong.

The Mahabharata teaches us that nobody is born evil. We all start out life as pure souls. Our experiences, our upbringing and our choices define us. Our lives are not always what they seem to be from the outside. Therefore, we must introspect- without knowing a person's private struggles, their setbacks and their unheard stories, is it wise to judge them?

# Mahabharata : A synopsis

*This is an attempt to summarise Mahabharata, a vast piece of literature, to help add context to this book. In order to understand the real story of Mahabharata and its complex world of characters and incidents, we urge you to read the many great books written on the subject by distinguished writers.*

You don't need a big torch to start a forest fire. Sometimes, a small spark is enough. The story of Mahabharata is an example of that. And the small spark? A case of wearing the wrong clothes.

Daughter of King Vrishaparvan and the princess of the Asuras, Sharmishta was close friends with her guru's daughter, Devayani. One day, they went swimming with their friends. But, by the time they decided to go back, it was dark. Suddenly aware of the howling animals, they haphazardly clothed themselves.

By accident, Devayani wore princess Sharmishta's silk sari. In anger, Sharmishta threw Devyani's cotton sari at her and pushed her into a dry well.

As luck would have it, King Yayati who was passing by, found her and helped her out, holding her right hand with his left. During those days, if a man held a woman's hand in this fashion, it symbolised marriage. Now that they were legally married, Devayani went home to prepare to leave for her marital home.

When her father, Guru Shukracharya found out what had happened, he demanded that princess Sharmishta go with Devayani to her marital home as her servant or else he would refuse to perform the yagnas required for their victory against the devas.

After weighing his chances, the King bid goodbye to his daughter, Sharmishta, with a heavy heart. His precious daughter, a princess, had overnight been turned into a servant.

Many years passed. King Yayati and his wife Devayani's first child, Yadu* was born. One day, while Devayani was pregnant with their second child, Turvasu, King Yayati came across Sharmishtha in the palace grounds. Enchanted by her royal demeanour, Yayati fathered three children with her- Anu, Druhyu and Puru.

*Krishna is a descendant of Yadu and belongs to a long line of kingmakers.

Years later, Devayani discovered her husband's betrayal and made her father, Guru Shukracharya curse King Yayati with old age. Upon much begging on the king's part, Shukracharya told him he could exchange his old age for his son's youth. Since only his son Puru agreed, Yayati cursed the rest of them, rendering them and their descendants incapable of ruling. Soon after, Yayati retired to the forest after restoring Puru's youth and naming him king.

A descendant of Puru was Kuru, who was blessed to become a wishing tree. When his time came, he refused to die. Indra blessed him, saying that his kingdom will go to heaven as well. When even that failed to convince him, Indra said anyone who dies on the battlefield of Kurukshetra will go to heaven.

Kuru accepted the boon but chose to remain as the wish-granting tree. Indra planted him in heaven where he remains forevermore.

One day, a descendant of Kuru, Shantanu, was walking along the Ganga and noticed a beautiful woman exiting from the water. It was love at first sight, and he asked her to marry him.

The woman told Shantanu she would leave if he questioned her actions or her past and her identity.

He agreed and they got married and had eight children. However, the woman drowned all of them. When she was about to drown the eighth one, Shantanu, who had been watching all this, finally stopped her.

"Are you a woman or a monster? What kind of mother kills her own children? I was too besotted with you to stop you, but I cannot let this happen any longer! What is wrong with you and give me my child!"

The woman listened to his tirade with a tired smile. When he had finally finished, she retreated into the water, dragging the very confused and bewildered king with her, holding her newborn son in her arms, and slowly, the water lifted them up, forming a kind of bubble around them.

"I am Ganga. Your children, our children, were the Vasus cursed to be born on Earth. They begged me to be their mother and keep their time on Earth short. I agreed. But this 8th one will remain. He will be returned to you on his 14th birthday."

With this, she disappeared and Shantanu found himself back in Hastinapura.

Fourteen years later, his son Devarata was indeed returned to him. One day, while hunting on the river, Shantanu smelled a beautiful fragrance. It was Satyavati, a fisher princess. He begged to marry her, but couldn't adhere to Satyavati's condition that Shantanu's son,

Devavrata, the crown prince and crown jewel, should never become the king. Shantanu was overcome with sadness at not being able to marry Satyavati.

When Devavrata discovered the reason for his father's grief , he agreed to both conditions that Satyavati now set- that Devavrata will never become the king and to avoid his children from sitting on the throne, he would never marry.

Since he took such terrible (bheeshan) vows, he was hailed as Bhishma.

Sathyavati married Shantanu and had two sons Chitrangada and Vichitraveerya, married to the princess Ambika and Ambalika respectively. When they both died prematurely, as per niyoga, Veda Vyasa fathered their children Pandu and Dhritarashtra.

When they grew up, Pandu was made the king of Hastinapur. He was married to Kunti and Madri. Dhritarashtra, though older, was not allowed to sit on the throne as he was blind. He was married to Gandhari.

Later, Pandu got inflicted by a terrible curse that if he touched a woman, he would die. He moved to the forest with his wives, with Dhritarashtra as regent ruling over Hastinapur. When Pandu passed away, Madri jumped into his funeral pyre, leaving behind her children, Nakula and Sahadeva, and Kunti and her sons Yudishtira, Bhima, and Arjuna. Yudishtira was the oldest.

The five boys called themselves the Pandavas. They moved to the palace to live with Dhritarashtra and his hundred sons, the Kauravas. The cousins were always fighting and a number of petty conflicts led to a full-scale eighteen-day war at the end of which the Pandavas emerged victorious after killing every last member of the Kauravas. The Pandavas were camping on the borders of the battlefield, as was the custom when their guru's son, Ashwatthama mistook their sons with their queen, Draupadi and killed them.

The Pandavas ruled for decades, until they decided to take the final journey up to swarga. All except Yudishtira died. He entered heaven, the only mortal to do so in human form, and ruled over 3 lokas with his deceased family by his side forevermore.

# About the author

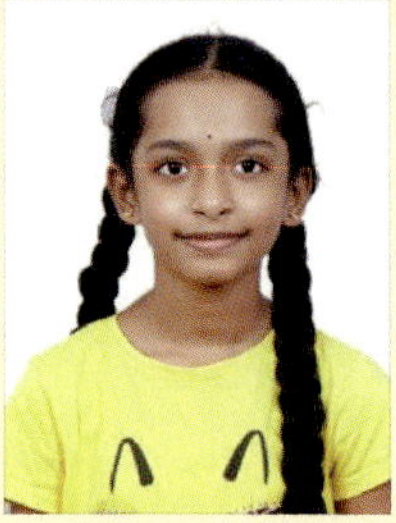

*Aashritha Surya Prakash is a 7th grade student of Vidyaniketan School, Bangalore. She enjoys maths and science as much as she does languages and history. She has been learning Bharatanatyam for 7 years and enjoys art and music. She started reading at the age of 6 and has been hooked onto books ever since. She loves all genres of books, whether it be science fiction, fantasy fiction, biographies, or mythology of any kind- Indian, Greek, roman, or norse!*

# Notes

# READER'S NOTES

How did you feel about these lesser celebrated characters of the Mahabharata?

Is there someone else from the epic that you would like to talk/think about?

Have your thoughts published at Bookosmia (smell of books) by sending to sara@bookosmia.com

# ABOUT CO-PUBLISHER

Bookosmia
Smell of Books

## Where EVERY Young Voice Matters

Share your thoughts as writings/ art/ audio/video etc and get digitally published for free, alongside young people from 150+ locations

Visit our website or write to sara@bookosmia.com

FEATURED ON:

WORKED WITH: